/14

5/17

exile: _____

R/BL: _____

R Points: _____

Poptropica®

POPTOPICS ★ REAL WORLD FACTS

Scary Monsters

by Tracey West

Poptropica
An Imprint of Penguin Group (USA) LLC

POPTROPICA
Published by the Penguin Group
Penguin Group (USA) LLC, 375 Hudson Street, New York, New York 10014, USA

USA | Canada | UK | Ireland | Australia | New Zealand | India | South Africa | China

penguin.com
A Penguin Random House Company

Photo credits: cover and page i: © TT/iStock/Thinkstock; page 7, 9: © James McQuillan/iStock/Thinkstock; page 10: (bedbug) © Smith Chetanachan/iStock/Thinkstock, (flea) © Carolina K. Smith, M.D./iStock/Thinkstock, (tick) © Henrik Larsson/iStock/Thinkstock; page 11: (mosquito) © Henrik Larsson/iStock/Thinkstock, (lamprey) © croreja/iStock/Thinkstock, (leeches) © Sergiy Goruppa/iStock/Thinkstock, (finch) © Johan_Sedig/iStock/Thinkstock; page 13: © Hans Proppe/iStock/Thinkstock; page 14: © Patricia Marroquin/iStock/Thinkstock; page 15: © Purestock/Purestock/Thinkstock; page 16: © KrivosheevV/iStock/Thinkstock; page 18: © Fernando Gregory Milan/iStock/Thinkstock; page 22: © Thinkstock/Stockbyte/Thinkstock; page 24: © pictore/iStock/Thinkstock; page 25 (Abigail Adams, Mark Twain) Courtesy of Library of Congress, Prints & Photographs Division, (Anne Boleyn) © Photos.com/Photos.com/Thinkstock; page 27: (flashlight) © Nikita Sobolkov/iStock/Thinkstock, (lit door) © Wayne Stadler/iStock/Thinkstock; page 28: © Carrie Winegarden/iStock/Thinkstock; page 29: (Flying Dutchman) © Artur Furmanek/Hemera/Thinkstock, (monument) © Purestock/Purestock/Thinkstock; page 31: © Chris Rogers/iStock/Thinkstock; page 35: © Chris Rogers/iStock/Thinkstock; page 45: © Kiril Stanchev/iStock/Thinkstock; page 47: (gargoyle) © Maria Bell/Hemera/Thinkstock, (dark forest) © Zacarias Pereira da Mata/iStock/Thinkstock; page 54: (toy gorilla) © joji/iStock/Thinkstock, (praying mantis) © tuk69tuk/iStock/Thinkstock; page 55: (gorilla) © hpboerman/iStock/Thinkstock, (toy monster) © andreapesce/iStock/Thinkstock.

ISBN 978-0-448-48048-0   10 9 8 7 6 5 4 3 2 1

Poptopics: Connecting Poptropica to the Real World

When you enter Poptropica, you can explore different times, countries, and even planets with the stroke of a keyboard. And while you might be able to do amazing things like battle robots and defy gravity, you should know that every Island is somehow connected to the real world.

This book takes a real-world look at the scary monsters in Poptropica. The Islands of Poptropica are crawling with creepy creatures. You'll find them in obvious places like **Vampire's Curse Island** and **Zomberry Island**, but they also pop up in unexpected places like **Shark Tooth Island**.

So wait, you might be asking, *are you saying that monsters are real?* Well, no—not exactly. But every monster you encounter is based on a story, myth, or legend from the real world. And in the case of some scary monsters, such as Bigfoot, there are people who swear that they're as real as it gets . . . but you can make up your own mind!

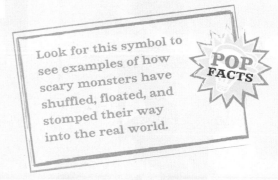

Look for this symbol to see examples of how scary monsters have shuffled, floated, and stomped their way into the real world.

POP FACTS

A Terrifying Trio

These three monsters have earned a place in the Horrifying Hall of Fame.

Back in the twentieth century, three monsters dominated the scene: the vampire, the werewolf, and Frankenstein's monster. They starred in movies, appeared in cartoons and comic books, and were the go-to costume for every kid on Halloween. Poptropicans love to dress up as these monsters, too.

Vampire

What they are: Once, they were human—until they died and became vampires. They sleep in coffins by day and rise at dusk to terrorize the living to satisfy their endless hunger for blood.

Why people like them: Vampires in movies are often portrayed as supernaturally gorgeous and romantic.

Werewolf

What they are: Werewolves are humans who transform into wolves when the moon is full, or who can transform into wolves at will.

Why people like them: Wolves bring out the wild side hidden in us all. They're strong, they're furry, and they run around free and howl at the moon.

Frankenstein's Monster

What he is: Dr. Frankenstein, a mad scientist, created him by sewing together the parts of various corpses. The doctor used electricity to bring the monster to life.

Why people like him: It's easy to feel sorry for this monster. He didn't ask to be created. He looks hideous, and everyone who sees him screams in fright. Anyone who has ever felt like an outsider can relate to him.

Still Scaring Strong!

All three of these monsters became popular way back in the 1930s and '40s, when audiences flocked to see movies about them. Now it's the twenty-first century, and people still can't get enough of vampires, werewolves, and Frankenstein's monster.

Portraits of classic monsters hang on the walls of the house in Poptropica's Haunted House mini-quest.

Vampires: A Bloody History

Tales of these creatures of the night are some of the oldest monster stories around.

Monster Stats

APPEARANCE: PALE SKIN, SHARP FANGS (SOMETIMES RETRACTABLE)

POWERS: IMMORTALITY, FLIGHT, CAN TRANSFORM INTO BATS OR WOLVES (BUT NOT WEREWOLVES)

DANGERS: WILL SUCK YOUR BLOOD (IF YOU'RE LUCKY, THEY'LL LEAVE YOU SOME)

WEAKNESSES: SUNLIGHT, CROSSES, HOLY WATER, GARLIC

QUIRKS: CAN'T CAST A SHADOW, CAN'T SEE THEIR REFLECTION IN A MIRROR

Ancient Evil

Some of the first legends of vampire-like creatures come from the ancient Greeks. They told stories of humans who were hungry for blood and attacked helpless people while they were sleeping.

In the Middle Ages, diseases like the plague spread through Europe, wiping out entire families. Stories spread about the dead coming to life to drink the blood of healthy humans and give them the plague as a result.

These stories continued into the 1700s, when the word "vampire" first popped up. The word probably originated in Serbia, where vampire legends were very popular. Around the same time, writers began to create stories and poems about vampires.

When Vampires Attack . . .

. . . there are several ways to keep them at bay. They are supposed to hate garlic, and won't go near a Christian cross. Dousing them with holy water will harm them. If you're being chased and you don't have any of those things, try to cross running water, like a creek or a river—vampires won't be able to follow. And if you scatter seeds or grains behind you, the vampire will be compelled to stop and count them all, buying you time.

If you must destroy a vampire, the stories say that a stake through the heart will do the trick. So will fire or decapitation. And sunlight is said to weaken vampires or even reduce them to a pile of ash.

In Vampire's Curse Island, you must make a potion using wolfsbane, mandrake root, and garlic if you want to defeat the vampire there.

Spotlight: Count Dracula

For centuries, he was the most famous vampire in history.

From the Mind of Bram Stoker

In Vampire's Curse Island, you will encounter Count Bram, a vampire with fangs, a fancy suit, and a cape. He is named after Bram Stoker, the Irish author of the novel *Dracula,* which was published in 1897.

Some scholars believe that to write the novel, Stoker took the old vampire legends and combined them with a real person: a Transylvanian prince named Vlad the Impaler. Born in 1431, he was famous for his cruelty to his enemies. He was nicknamed "Dracula," meaning "son of a dragon," because his father belonged to a military organization called the Order of the Dragon.

Dracula was not the first book ever about vampires, but it quickly became the most famous. Stoker's story and character went on to inspire books, movies, TV shows, and more.

Dracula Rules

Most of the "rules" we know about vampires come from Bram Stoker's book. Here are some of them:

* Count Dracula could control the minds of others, control the weather, and transform into animals.
* He was a wealthy aristocrat from a noble family, so the red-lined cape, expensive suit, and medal around the neck that he wore were typical for someone of his station in life. For decades, it was the main costume of vampires everywhere.
* Because he was a count, he lived in a castle. Many vampires after him lived in spooky castles, too.
* Count Dracula couldn't enter a home unless he was invited and couldn't cross water unless someone carried him.

Due to a childhood illness, Bram Stoker didn't walk until he was seven years old. He went on to become a college athlete and even played football (soccer) at Trinity College in Dublin, Ireland.

POP CULTURE

Vampires through Time

Take a look at how cape-wearing vampires transformed into sparkling bad boys over the years.

1922: IN THE MOVIE *NOSFERATU*, MYSTERIOUS ACTOR MAX SCHRECK PLAYED ONE OF THE CREEPIEST-LOOKING VAMPIRES EVER SEEN.

1931: ACTOR BELA LUGOSI BROUGHT BRAM STOKER'S CHARACTER TO LIFE (WELL, UNDEAD LIFE) IN THE MOVIE *DRACULA* (HE HAD ALSO PERFORMED IN THE BROADWAY VERSION OF THE NOVEL FOUR YEARS EARLIER).

1954: A TV HORROR HOST NAMED VAMPIRA (PLAYED BY MAILA NURMI) PROVED THAT WOMEN COULD BE VAMPIRES, TOO.

1964: THE POPULAR TV SHOW *THE MUNSTERS* FEATURED A MONSTER FAMILY WITH A VAMPIRE MOM NAMED LILY.

1992: WE FIRST MET BUFFY THE VAMPIRE SLAYER IN THE MOVIE THAT INSPIRED THE POPULAR TELEVISION SERIES ABOUT A CHEERLEADER WHO BATTLES VAMPIRES.

1972: ON *SESAME STREET*, THE MUPPET COUNT VON COUNT HELPED KIDS LEARN HOW TO—WHAT ELSE?—COUNT!

2008: MOVIEGOERS FLOCKED TO SEE THE FIRST INSTALLMENT IN STEPHENIE MEYER'S HUGELY POPULAR VAMPIRE SERIES, *THE TWILIGHT SAGA*, ON-SCREEN. THEY SWOONED OVER VAMPIRE EDWARD CULLEN, WHO SPARKLES IN THE SUNLIGHT AND NORMALLY WEARS JEANS AND BUTTON-DOWN SHIRTS.

Meet the Slayers

* Cactus Von Garlic: He appears in the bonus quest for Vampire's Curse Island wearing a metal band around his neck to prevent vampire bites. He eventually experiences a change of heart when he learns that vampires can be cured.
* Dr. Abraham Van Helsing: He first appeared in Bram Stoker's *Dracula* as a doctor who discovers that Count Dracula is a vampire. He leads the group of men who track down the count and kill him. A reimagined version of him appears in the 2004 film *Van Helsing* as a human with supernatural abilities to kill monsters.
* Buffy the Vampire Slayer: Buffy is a teenager who discovers that she is the next in a long line of vampire slayers. Creator Joss Whedon told her story in a 1992 movie and then a long-running TV series starring Sarah Michelle Gellar as Buffy.

IN POPTROPICA, YOU CAN FIND VAMPIRE COSTUMES MODELED AFTER MODERN VAMPIRES LIKE THE ONES IN *TWILIGHT*.

Nature's Bloodsuckers

Not all bloodsuckers are fictional. These creepy creatures are real!

Vampire bats: There are three species of bats that drink blood: the common vampire bat, white-winged vampire bat, and hairy-legged vampire bat. They mostly feed on farm animals such as cows and pigs. That's because when they fly out late at night, humans are usually indoors.

Bedbugs: Like vampires, bedbugs prefer to come out at night in search of a meal: usually the blood of the nearest human. A female bedbug can lay as many as six hundred eggs in one year, which is partly why these pests have become such a huge problem in recent years.

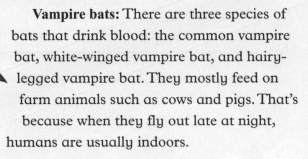

Fleas: After a bedbug bites you, it will go off to digest. Fleas aren't so polite. They will live on their hosts—mammals and birds—feeding off their blood.

Ticks: The American dog tick needs several feedings of blood to grow. After a female feeds on a host (dogs and humans are favorites) for several days, she'll drop off and lay eggs that hatch into six-legged larvae. The larvae feed

on more blood and then morph into nymphs with eight legs. They feed again, and then they shed their skins and become adults.

Female mosquito: That's right, those pesky mosquitoes that bite you are all females. She needs the protein in blood to make sure her eggs will grow properly.

Lamprey: A close-up look at a lamprey's mouth is guaranteed to cause nightmares. This eel-like creature's round maw contains a spiral of teeth designed for sucking blood and tissue from its host.

Leeches: These members of the worm family can live on land and in water. Leeches suck blood by first biting their victims. Chemicals in its saliva numb the pain and also prevent blood from clotting.

Galápagos finches: Bloodsucking birds? This phenomenon has only been seen in the Galápagos Islands. When food is scarce, certain tiny finches will hop up behind larger seabirds called boobies. They will peck at a booby's skin until blood flows, and then drink it up.

Howling at the Moon

Werewolves are monsters that bring out the beast in all of us.

Monster Stats

APPEARANCE: LIKE A WOLF, ONLY BIGGER AND SCARIER; SOMETIMES WALKS ON TWO LEGS

POWERS: IN SOME LEGENDS, A HUMAN WILL ONLY TURN INTO A WEREWOLF WHEN THE MOON IS FULL—WHETHER THEY WANT TO OR NOT. OTHER LEGENDS TELL OF POWERFUL WEREWOLVES WHO CAN TRANSFORM AT WILL.

DANGERS: THEY WILL EAT YOU. IF YOU SURVIVE THEIR BITE, YOU WILL BECOME A WEREWOLF, TOO.

WEAKNESSES: SILVER BULLETS OR WEAPONS (AND PROBABLY FLEAS, TOO)

QUIRKS: WHEN KILLED, A WEREWOLF WILL RETURN TO HUMAN FORM

A Primal Fear

You're walking through Vampire's Curse Island. It's a dark night. Lightning flashes. Suddenly, out of the dark, a creature with glowing red eyes lunges at you! It's a wolf! Your heart pounds as you scramble to get away.

Humans have been terrified of wolves for thousands of years. These deadly predators roamed the forests at night, howling and killing wild game and livestock.

The idea that humans could transform into wolves probably started way back in ancient Greece. One myth says that Zeus, the king of the gods, punished a cruel king named Lycaon by turning him into a wolf.

Stories of werewolves became popular in the Middle Ages. The word "wer" is an Old English word meaning "man." In sixteenth-century France, many men were tried and convicted of being werewolves.

The Boy Who Fought the Beast

Between 1764 and 1767, the French countryside was terrorized by a giant wolf that reportedly attacked two hundred people, killing 113 of them. Stories sprang up that the "Beast of Gévaudan" must be a werewolf.

One of the humans to face the beast was twelve-year-old Jacques Portefaix, a shepherd. When the wolf attacked, Jacques defended his friends with a sharp stick. He got three hundred *livres* (old-school French money) and was sent away to a nice school as a reward.

Lycanthropy is a mental disorder that causes some people to believe they're wolves.

POP SCIENCE

Frankenstein's Monster

One of the most chilling monsters of all time sprang from the mind of a teenage girl.

Monster Stats

APPEARANCE: IN THE NOVEL, THE MONSTER IS DESCRIBED AS EIGHT FEET TALL, WITH TIGHT YELLOW SKIN, LONG BLACK HAIR, AND BLACK LIPS

POWERS: UNUSUALLY STRONG

DANGERS: GETS ANGRY EASILY

WEAKNESSES: THE SAME AS ANY OTHER HUMAN

It's Alive!

This famous exclamation is shouted by Dr. Frankenstein when his creature comes to life in the 1931 film *Frankenstein*. Based on the book by Mary Shelley (see page 16), the movie was a hit, and people became fascinated with the monster. He was played by actor Boris Karloff, and the image of him in the monster's makeup is the most famous one ever of the monster.

14

Here Comes the Bride

The film *Bride of Frankenstein* came out in 1935, and introduced a new creature created by Dr. Frankenstein to keep his monster company. It backfired when she was brought to life and screamed at the sight of the monster. With her signature white gown and lightning-streaked hair, the Bride of Frankenstein has become almost more famous than her intended mate.

It Was a Dark and Stormy Night

It was the summer of 1816, and nineteen-year-old Mary Wollstonecraft Godwin was on a holiday with her fiancé,

the poet Percy Bysshe Shelley, and their friends, including another poet, Lord Byron. The weather was cold and rainy, and after reading ghost stories, they challenged each other to see who could write the scariest tale.

Mary challenged herself to create a story that would "make the reader dread to look 'round, to curdle the blood, and quicken the beatings of the heart." Before the summer ended, she started to see images in her mind of "the hideous phantasm of a man stretched out, and then, on the working of some powerful engine, show signs of life, and stir with an uneasy, half-vital motion."

Two years later, she had married Shelley and published

MARY SHELLEY NEVER NAMED THE MONSTER IN THE NOVEL. OVER THE YEARS, PEOPLE HAVE STARTED CALLING THE MONSTER "FRANKENSTEIN" AFTER HIS CREATOR.

her novel, *Frankenstein; or, The Modern Prometheus.* In it, she tells the tale of Dr. Victor Frankenstein, a scientist obsessed with finding the key to eternal life. He creates a monster from the bodies of corpses. The monster is intelligent but shunned for his hideous appearance, and he responds with violence.

YOU'LL MEET A FEW MAD SCIENTISTS IN POPTROPICA, LIKE THE INFAMOUS DR. HARE.

The Undead

What's scarier, a zombie or a ghost? Both monsters used to be among the living, and now they're dead. Ghosts no longer have bodies and have a habit of haunting the places they used to live. Zombies still have bodies—although a bit rotten—but they've lost all human intelligence and only exist to eat the brains of living humans.

It's a tough question. Nobody wants to get their brains eaten. But while it's theoretically possible to outrun a zombie, can you ever really get away from a ghost?

If you want to explore this question further, Poptropica can help you. For a zombie fix, head over to Zomberry Island, where you'll have to dodge hordes of ghouls to try to find a cure for the plague that's turning everyone into zombies. On Ghost Story Island, you'll use high-tech equipment to prove the existence of ghosts in several haunted places.

You might want to visit both of these Islands with the lights on. Some pretty spooky scares await you there!

Braaaiiiiins . . .

They're dead. No, they're alive! And they want to eat your brains.

Monster Stats

APPEARANCE: A ZOMBIE IS A WALKING CORPSE, SO IT'S NOT PRETTY TO LOOK AT. EXPECT ROTTING FLESH, EXPOSED BONES, AND TATTERED CLOTHING.

POWERS: IN SOME STORIES, THEY ARE PORTRAYED AS BEING EXTREMELY FAST

DANGERS: ZOMBIES GAIN STRENGTH IN NUMBERS. YOU MIGHT BE ABLE TO OUTRUN ONE SLOW ZOMBIE. BUT ZOMBIES TEND TO TRAVEL IN LARGE GROUPS. IF YOU'RE SURROUNDED, THERE'S NOT MUCH YOU CAN DO.

WEAKNESSES: TO DESTROY A ZOMBIE, YOU MUST DESTROY ITS BRAIN

It Began in Haiti

The original zombie was part of the Haitian religion Vodou, or Voodoo. A *zombi* was a dead person who was revived after being buried, and had to do the bidding of the person who brought him back.

In 1929, an explorer named William Seabrook wrote a book called *The Magic Island* after visiting Haiti, and described the Vodou religion. Zombie movies popped up after that, featuring the Haitian *zombi*. But these poor souls are very different than the zombies that are popular today.

The Father of the Zombie Craze

On Zomberry Island, you'll meet Dr. G. Romero, a scientist trying to come up with a cure for the Zomberry Plague. He's named after George Romero, a film director who helped start the twentieth-century zombie craze.

In 1968, he turned the tables on zombie mythology with his film *Night of the Living Dead.* In it, nobody is sure why the bodies of the recently dead are coming to life. Radiation from a space probe is suspected. The word "zombie" is never used, but the slow-moving, brain-hungry creatures could be nothing else. Romero went on to make more zombie movies, and others quickly followed. Over the next several decades, zombies appeared in music videos, video games, books, and more.

BESIDES RADIATION, OTHER REASONS FOR IMAGINED ZOMBIE OUTBREAKS INCLUDE CHEMICAL POISONING, AND A PLAGUE OR VIRUS. GENERALLY, IT IS THOUGHT THAT IF A ZOMBIE BITES YOU, YOU WILL BECOME A ZOMBIE YOURSELF.

Ghosts

People tell great stories about them—and they make for a pretty easy Halloween costume, too.

Monster Stats

APPEARANCE: IT DEPENDS ON THE GHOST. IT MIGHT APPEAR AS A SEE-THROUGH VERSION OF A HUMAN, A DARK SHADOW, OR A GLOWING ORB. OTHER GHOSTS MIGHT NOT BE SEEN AT ALL, BUT YOU'LL KNOW THEY'RE THERE BECAUSE YOU'LL FEEL THEM, HEAR THEM, OR SEE THEM MOVE SOMETHING.

POWERS: WALKING THROUGH WALLS, APPEARING AND DISAPPEARING

DANGERS: GHOSTS DON'T USUALLY CAUSE HARM TO THE PEOPLE THEY HAUNT, BUT THEY DO SCARE THEM SILLY

What's in a Ghost?

A ghost, basically, is the soul or spirit of someone who has died. For some reason, the spirit does not want to leave earth to pass into the next realm, so it stays here. What does it do after that? Well, that's when things get more complicated. Ghosts have different ways of making their presence known.

Ghosts You Can See

Some ghosts appear to the living in some form:

* A see-through version of their former selves
* A glowing orb of light
* A shadow on the wall or in the corner

Ghosts You Can't See

Some ghosts can't be seen, but we know they're there.

* A poltergeist is a type of ghost that throws objects around and breaks things. They are sometimes referred to as "knocking ghosts," which comes from the German words *poltern*, which means "to make sound," and *Geist*, which means "ghost." They are usually present when there is a teenager in the family, leading some scientists to believe that they are not ghosts at all but some kind of adolescent energy force.
* Some ghosts make themselves known by opening and shutting doors or moving objects around the house.
* Other ghosts can only be heard. People have reported hearing low, sad moans. Others hear footsteps that travel the same area over and over.

Famous Phantoms

Meet some famous folks who became historical haunters in the afterlife.

Benjamin Franklin: A statue of Franklin stands outside the American Philosophical Society Library in Philadelphia. People have reported that the statue comes to life, and Franklin starts dancing!

Dolley Madison: She was the wife of James Madison, who became America's fourth president in 1809. The Rose Garden in the White House was her pride and joy, and when workers tried to dig it up about a hundred years later, she appeared to them and told them to back off. The garden is still blooming to this day.

Abraham Lincoln: Many people have claimed to see the specter of our sixteenth president in the White House. When Franklin Roosevelt was president, Queen Wilhelmina of the Netherlands came for a visit. She heard a knock on her door at midnight. When she opened it, she saw the ghost of Abraham Lincoln in his top hat—and fainted.

Abigail Adams: Another phantom First Lady, she was married to John Adams, the first president to live in the White House. When they moved in, in 1800, the house was still under construction, and Abigail needed to find the best place to do laundry. That may be why her ghost is seen with her arms extended, as if she is holding a laundry basket, and hurrying toward the East Room.

Mark Twain: This humorist and author is best known for novels including *The Adventures of Tom Sawyer* and *The Adventures of Huckleberry Finn*. He lived in Greenwich Village, New York, for over a year, and his ghost is said to haunt the apartment building to this day.

Anne Boleyn: She was the second wife of England's King Henry VIII. When she was unable to provide him with a male heir, he had her charged with treason and other crimes. She was executed at the Tower of London in 1536. Her ghost has been sighted at the tower as well as in her childhood home and other locations.

Ghost Busters!

On the search for a specter? You'll need some high-tech equipment to do the job.

On Ghost Story Island, a Poptropican named Jane will provide you with a thermal sensor, thermometer, and EMF detector to help you locate ghosts. These are just some of the tools that professional ghost hunters use. Here's what the pros use when they're tracking phantoms:

Digital Infrared Thermometer: Researchers have reported that the temperature in a space can suddenly become very cold or hot when a spirit is present. The thermometer can detect these changes.

EMF Meter: This device detects changes in magnetic fields produced by the flow of AC electrical currents. Appliances such as your refrigerator give out EMFs (electromagnetic fields)—and so do ghosts, researchers believe. This meter helps ghost hunters tell if the EMFs around them are caused by a phantom or a fridge.

EVP Recorder: EVP stands for Electric Voice Phenomena. Researchers have found that tape recorders can pick up ghostly sounds that are not heard by the human ear—but can be heard when the tape is played back. This device also records sounds that crop up in magnetic fields.

Flashlight/Night-Vision Goggles: Ghosts seem to prefer the nightlife, so these useful tools will help you see your way around when you're hunting them in the dark.

Full Spectrum Camcorder: In a pinch, you can always record ghostly phenomena with a standard digital recorder. The pros use this one, which can also record wavelengths of light that can't be seen with the human eye.

Laser Grid Scope: Sometimes, a ghost appears quickly or only as a shadow. This device projects a pattern of green dots onto a surface (like a blank wall, for example), so if something supernatural does whiz by, it can be seen more easily.

Motion Sensor: Ghosts aren't always visible. So how can you tell if one is in the same room with you? The motion detector will tell you if something in the room is moving—besides you.

Is Your House Haunted?

Those groans you hear at night could just be the wind . . . or something from another realm.

In Ghost Story Island and the Haunted House mini-quest, you'll explore a ghostly manor, a haunted inn, and other phantom-plagued places. Be on the lookout for these phenomena, which might indicate there is a ghost nearby:

- Objects move on their own.
- Spiders weave warnings into their webs.
- A spooky fog rises up.
- Doors open and shut by themselves.
- You hear strange moaning sounds—but you're sure you're alone.
- The people in portraits follow you with their eyes.

Real-Life Haunted Places

Winchester Mystery House, San Jose, California:

Nobody can say for sure why Sarah Winchester built this bizarre house, which contains numerous secret passages, stairways that go nowhere, and doors that open up to steep drops outside. She had the home built after the death of her husband, Oliver, inventor of the Winchester rifle. The story goes that she thought she was being haunted by the spirits of all the souls that had been killed by the guns, and she built the house to confuse them and keep herself safe.

Belcourt Castle, Newport, Rhode Island: This magnificent mansion is filled with antique armor, and the ghosts who haunt it are believed to be the men who once wore the armor. The castle also contains a mirror that doesn't allow you to see your reflection—but if you look in it, you'll see ghostly images moving back and forth.

The Flying Dutchman: Legends of this haunted merchant ship stem from the seventeenth century. Its crew is doomed to sail forever. The ship sometimes appears as a hazy light on the waves, and if you see it, it means bad luck is on the way.

Gettysburg, Pennsylvania: The tragic Battle of Gettysburg took place from July 1 to July 3, 1863. There were more than 50,000 casualties during those three days.

Ever since then, countless visitors have reported hearing, seeing, or being touched by ghosts in Gettysburg. The most famous is a sentry who watches over the cupola at the top of Pennsylvania Hall at Gettysburg College. A soldier, he is often seen pacing back and forth with a rifle in his hands.

Cryptids: The Debate Still Rages

If you've ever visited Cryptids Island, then you know a little something about cryptids. These are creatures that some people believe are real, because there have been many reports of seeing them. However, nobody has ever captured one or taken a conclusive photo or video of one. So others believe that cryptids are just stories and aren't real at all.

On Cryptids Island, a wealthy man named Harold Mews is offering a big reward for proof of the existence of a cryptid. In the real world, cryptid-hunting is a big business. TV shows follow teams around the world as they use expensive equipment to search for proof.

So far, only one cryptid's existence has been proven: the giant squid. For the others, the search will go on—and so will the arguments.

Possible yeti track

REWARD

?

$1,000,000

FOR IRREFUTABLE PROOF OF THE EXISTENCE OF A CRYPTID

Search the world and bring your proof to Harold Mews to claim your reward.

The word *cryptid* comes from the Greek word *krypto*, which means "hidden." The study of cryptids is called cryptozoology.

POP VOCABULARY

Creatures of the Deep

Sail the seas of Poptropica and you'll encounter sea monsters of all shapes and sizes. Here's a look at some of these legendary beasts and their real-life counterparts.

SEA MONSTER

GREAT BOOGA SHARK

THIS GIANT BEAST WITH A WEAKNESS FOR COCONUTS TERRORIZES THE RESIDENTS OF SHARK TOOTH ISLAND. ONLY A SLEEPING POTION CAN TAME HIM.

GIANT PUFFER FISH

IN THE SEAS OF SKULLDUGGERY ISLAND, YOU'LL ENCOUNTER PUFFER FISH AS BIG AS HOT-AIR BALLOONS.

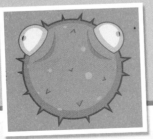

REAL-LIFE MONSTER

GREAT WHITE SHARK

THESE FEARED PREDATORS HAVE APPROXIMATELY SEVEN ROWS OF SHARP TEETH, CAN SWIM AS FAST AS THIRTY-FIVE MILES PER HOUR, AND CAN GROW AS BIG AS TWENTY FEET LONG AND WEIGH AS MUCH AS SEVEN THOUSAND POUNDS. THEIR ONLY PREDATOR IS THE HUMAN, WHO THEY ARE OCCASIONALLY KNOWN TO ATTACK. CURRENTLY, THEY ARE LISTED AS A THREATENED SPECIES.

PUFFER FISH

ALSO CALLED BLOWFISH, THEY BELONG TO A FAMILY OF FISH THAT CAN INFLATE WITH AIR WHEN THEY'RE DISTURBED. SOME CAN GET AS LARGE AS THREE FEET, BUT MOST ARE SMALLER. THEY CAN BE DEADLY, THOUGH, IF YOU DON'T CLEAN THEM CAREFULLY BEFORE EATING THEM. THEIR INTERNAL ORGANS CONTAIN A HIGHLY TOXIC POISON.

SEA MONSTER

GIANT CRAB

THE WATERS OF SKULLDUGGERY ISLAND CONTAIN CRABS AS LARGE AS YOUR PIRATE SHIP.

BIG TENTACLED CREATURE

THE CREATURE WITH TENTACLES THAT ATTACKS YOU IN SKULLDUGGERY ISLAND COULD BE A GIANT OCTOPUS OR MAYBE A LEGENDARY SEA CREATURE KNOWN AS A KRAKEN. STORIES OF THE KRAKEN ORIGINATED IN SCANDINAVIA, WHERE TALES ARE TOLD OF A GREAT BEAST THAT DRAGGED SHIPS DOWN BENEATH THE WAVES AND ATE THE UNLUCKY SAILORS ON BOARD.

IN LAB TESTS, THE PACIFIC OCTOPUS CAN OPEN JARS AND SOLVE MAZES!

REAL-LIFE MONSTER

GIANT SPIDER CRAB

THE REAL-LIFE GIANT SPIDER CRAB LIVES IN THE WATERS OF THE PACIFIC OCEAN, NEAR JAPAN. IT CAN GROW AS LARGE AS TWELVE FEET WIDE FROM CLAW TO CLAW, BUT ITS BODY IS ABOUT FIFTEEN INCHES ACROSS. THEY ARE NOT KNOWN TO ATTACK HUMANS.

GIANT PACIFIC OCTOPUS

WHILE THE COMMON OCTOPUS GROWS TO ABOUT FOUR FEET ACROSS, THIS SPECIES CAN REACH THIRTY FEET AND A WHOPPING SIX HUNDRED POUNDS. THEY PREFER SEAFOOD TO HUMANS, AND SOME HAVE BEEN KNOWN TO USE THEIR SHARP MOUTH TO RIP UP SHARKS.

He's Big, Hairy, and Hard to Catch

Bigfoot creatures go by many names, and they can be found all over the world.

These creatures all have some things in common. They are thought to be half human and half ape. They're tall and walk on two legs. They're covered with hair or fur, and smell like rotten eggs. They leave huge footprints in their wake, and their howls sound like nothing ever heard before. Take a look at the four main versions of this beast:

Monster Stats

BIGFOOT/SASQUATCH
LIVES IN: THE FORESTS OF NORTH AMERICA
HEIGHT: 6 TO 15 FEET TALL
FOOTPRINTS: 2 FEET LONG AND 8 INCHES WIDE
FUR: REDDISH BROWN
SIGHTINGS: THE FIRST BIGFOOT PRINTS ARE THOUGHT TO HAVE BEEN FOUND BY AN EXPLORER NAMED DAVID THOMPSON IN 1811.
THE MOST FAMOUS SIGHTING WAS A FILM OF A BIGFOOT WALKING IN CALIFORNIA IN 1967, ALTHOUGH REPORTS SUGGEST THAT THIS WAS FAKED.
THE WORD "SASQUATCH" COMES FROM A WORD IN THE LANGUAGE OF NATIVES OF THE PACIFIC NORTHWEST. IT MEANS "WILD MAN."

YETI

SOMETIMES CALLED: THE ABOMINABLE SNOWMAN

LIVES IN: THE HIMALAYAN MOUNTAIN RANGE IN NEPAL, ABOVE THE SNOW LINE

FUR: REDDISH BROWN OR GRAY, ALTHOUGH SOMETIMES SHOWN AS WHITE

FOOTPRINTS: ABOUT 1 FOOT WIDE AND 1 1/2 FEET LONG

SIGHTINGS: THE NATIVE PEOPLE OF NEPAL TOLD TALES OF A SUPERSTRONG, FUR-COVERED CREATURE THEY THOUGHT WAS A DEMON. IT'S SAID THAT WHEN SIR EDMUND HILLARY CLIMBED MOUNT EVEREST IN 1953, HE WAS GIVEN A YETI SKULL THAT HAD BEEN KEPT BY MONKS. MANY SPECULATE THAT THE SKULL ACTUALLY BELONGED TO A MOUNTAIN GOAT.

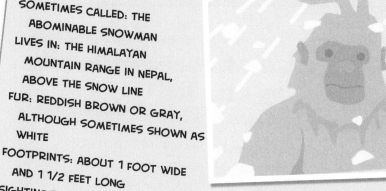

YOWIE

LIVES IN: THE MOUNTAINOUS REGIONS OF SOUTHEASTERN AUSTRALIA

HEIGHT: AS TALL AS 6 TO 10 FEET, BUT CAN BE AS SMALL AS 4 FEET

FUR: LIGHT BROWN, REDDISH BROWN, GRAY, OR BLACK

SIGHTINGS: NATIVE ABORIGINES HAVE TOLD STORIES OF THIS BEAST FOR AGES; THE FIRST SIGHTING BY A SETTLER WAS REPORTED IN A NEWSPAPER IN 1790.

Loch Ness Monster

Is "Nessie" a dinosaur, a delusion—or something else?

Monster Stats

APPEARANCE: A LARGE WATER CREATURE WITH A BIG BODY,
   FLIPPERS, A LONG NECK, AND A SMALL HEAD
LENGTH: 40 TO 50 FEET
LIVES IN: LOCH NESS, A LARGE, DEEP LAKE IN SCOTLAND

What Is Nessie?

A creature of Nessie's description was reported as early as the year 565 AD, when Columbia, an Irish saint, said he saw it at the funeral of one of its victims. Sightings became more frequent in the twentieth century, when a new road started to bring lots of tourists to the loch.

In 1933, a man named Mr. Spicer and his wife reported seeing a creature with a long neck and big body cross the road in front of their car. It held an animal in its jaws. After this was reported in the newspaper, many people became interested in trying to sight the Loch Ness Monster.

The excitement swelled in 1934 when a British physician took a photo that resembled the description of the monster. Researchers debated this photo for years, and in 1994, a ninety-three-year-old man admitted that he had taken part in a hoax. The monster in the photo was a toy submarine with the head of a sea serpent.

That hasn't stopped researchers from continuing their search for Nessie. They have explored the depths of the loch in submarines using sonar equipment but have not yet found definitive proof that it exists.

Nessie's Cousins

"Champy" from Lake Champlain, USA
"Skrimsi" from Grimsey, Iceland
"Ogopogo" from Okanogan Lake, Canada

Loch Ness Monster?

The descriptions of Nessie resemble some kind of plesiosaur, a type of water-dwelling reptile with a long neck that lived from the end of the Triassic period 220 million years ago until the end of the Cretaceous period 65 million years ago. Could some have survived in Loch Ness? Some researchers speculate that the lake would not have enough food to feed a colony of plesiosaurs.

El Chupacabra

Lock up your farm animals! They're the favorite treat of this creepy cryptid.

Monster Stats

APPEARANCE: A DOG-LIKE CREATURE WITH A LONG SNOUT, LARGE FANGS, AND LEATHERY OR SCALY SKIN. SOME REPORTS SAY THAT IT WALKS ON TWO LEGS, AND HAS THREE TOES ON ITS FEET AND HANDS, GLOWING RED EYES, AND SPIKES ON ITS BACK.

HEIGHT: 4 TO 5 FEET TALL

LIVES IN: MAINLY LATIN AMERICA

DANGERS: NO HUMAN ATTACKS HAVE BEEN REPORTED, BUT FARM ANIMALS SUCH AS SHEEP AND GOATS ARE SAID TO HAVE HAD THE BLOOD SUCKED OUT OF THEM BY THIS CREATURE. THAT IS WHY IT'S CALLED EL CHUPACABRA, WHICH MEANS "THE GOAT SUCKER."

A Thoroughly Modern Monster

Unlike most cryptids, stories about El Chupacabra only started cropping up in modern times, in the late twentieth century. The first report was believed to have been made by a farmer in Puerto Rico in 1995. He said that three of his sheep had been killed by a creature that left puncture wounds on their bodies and drained their blood.

A few months later, a woman gave the first eyewitness account to a newspaper, describing a beast that walked on two legs and had spikes down its back. There was only one problem—the creature she described was a lot like one from a horror movie, *Species*.

That may explain why, in later stories, the description changed to something resembling more of a dog or coyote. Researchers labeled the case closed when they realized that the "monster" was, in most cases, a coyote afflicted with a disease called mange, which left the coyote with scaly skin and a frightening appearance.

Still, there are many believers who think this goat-sucking cryptid is still out there. Are you one of them?

The Jersey Devil

Here's proof that the cast of *Jersey Shore* isn't the most frightening thing to come from the Garden State.

Monster Stats

APPEARANCE: TALLER THAN A HUMAN, WITH HORNS, CLAWS, HOOVES, A HORSE-LIKE FACE, WINGS, AND GLOWING RED EYES

LIVES IN: NEW JERSEY

DANGERS: ATTACKS AND TERRIFIES HUMANS

Mother Leeds's Baby Boy

The year is 1735. Deep in the Pine Barrens of New Jersey, a woman named Mother Leeds is about to give birth to her thirteenth child. She's not thrilled to have so many children, so she curses the baby before it is born.

Legend says that the cursed baby sprang from her loins and then immediately transformed into a monster. It went on a rampage, flew up the chimney, and has been terrorizing residents of New Jersey ever since.

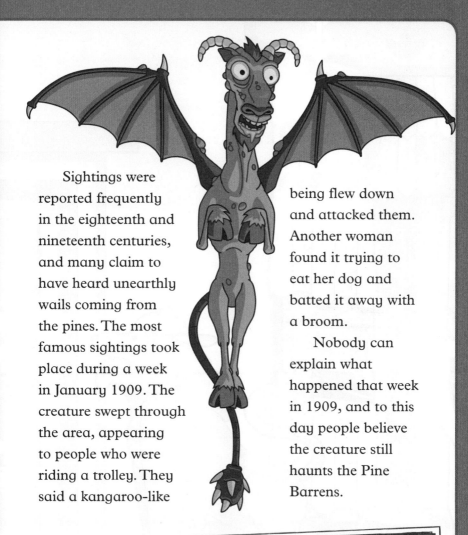

Sightings were reported frequently in the eighteenth and nineteenth centuries, and many claim to have heard unearthly wails coming from the pines. The most famous sightings took place during a week in January 1909. The creature swept through the area, appearing to people who were riding a trolley. They said a kangaroo-like being flew down and attacked them. Another woman found it trying to eat her dog and batted it away with a broom.

Nobody can explain what happened that week in 1909, and to this day people believe the creature still haunts the Pine Barrens.

The Pine Barrens of New Jersey stretch across more than a million acres and seven counties in this small state. The area is known for its sandy soil and forests of a species of the pitch pine tree called a "pygmy" pine. Much of the area is not developed, making it an ideal home for cryptids.

POP
GEOGRAPHY

Bunyip

Monster Stats

APPEARANCE: TALL, STOUT BODY, WITH A FACE LIKE A DOG, THE BILL OF A DUCK, FLIPPERS, A HORSE'S TAIL, DARK FUR, AND HORNS OR TUSKS

HEIGHT: 12 TO 13 FEET

LIVES IN: THE WATERS OF AUSTRALIA AND TASMANIA

DANGERS: ATTACKS AND TERRIFIES HUMANS

The Monster from Down Under

The Aborigines first told tales of the bunyip, which they thought to be an evil spirit. They said that the creature would not appear to non-natives of Australia, but settlers became fascinated with the legends about this cryptid.

The bunyip lives in fresh water: places like creeks, shallow lakes, and swamps. In the nineteenth century, newspapers started reporting bunyip sightings, but some speculated that those might just have been seals that swam upstream.

Australian Aborigines have lived in Australia for at least fifty thousand years. They are a society of hunters and gatherers that still use these practices in modern times.

POP HISTORY

Kappa

Monster Stats

APPEARANCE: ABOUT THE SIZE OF A CHILD, THE KAPPA HAS
BEEN DESCRIBED IN MANY DIFFERENT WAYS. IT HAS THE
BODY OF A FROG, AND A TURTLE'S SHELL AND BEAK, AND
WALKS ON TWO LEGS. THERE'S AN INDENT IN THE TOP OF
ITS HEAD THAT HOLDS WATER. IF THE WATER SPILLS OUT,
THE CREATURE WILL LOSE ITS POWER.

LIVES IN: THE WATERS OF JAPAN

DANGERS: PLAYS MISCHIEVOUS PRANKS, BUT MAY
ALSO TRY TO DROWN OR KIDNAP YOU

LIKES: CUCUMBERS

Japan's Water Spirit

If you visit a pond in
Japan, you might see a sign
with a picture of a Kappa on
it, warning you that one lives
there. This water creature has
long been a part of Japanese
mythology. Some think
that Kappa sightings might
actually be that of a giant
salamander called a *hanzaki*.
These amphibians can grow
to five feet long.

YOU MAY HAVE RUN INTO
A KAPPA ON RED DRAGON
ISLAND.
HE IS VERY MISCHIEVOUS AND
ELUDES YOUR TRAPS UNTIL
YOU FINALLY SNARE HIM.

Scary Fairies

"What's so scary about fairies?" you might be wondering. They're cute little things with wings, and live in flowers, and grant wishes, right? Well, their history is more complicated than that.

Stories about fairy creatures go back thousands of years and appear in cultures all over the world. There isn't just one type of fairy—there are hundreds, if not more. What they all pretty much have in common is that (a) they're not human; (b) they live in a separate world, kind of like another dimension, but they can travel to our world; and (c) they have unusual abilities or magical powers.

In Twisted Thicket Island, you'll meet some fairies on the scary side. That's not unusual; in fact, historically, fairies have been divided into two groups: good fairies and bad fairies.

Good Fairies

Also known as: the Seelie Court

"Seelie" means "blessed," and the fairies in this group are said to be kind to humans. They are beautiful to look at and will help with chores or give food to the poor. But even good fairies have a dark side: if you insult them in any way, they will punish you.

Bad Fairies

Also known as: the Unseelie Court

These "unblessed" fairies are always up to no good. Included in their ranks are the Sluagh, undead spirits that hover above earth and snatch unsuspecting victims into their clutches. Fairies that live alone and give humans a hard time are also included in this group—like the Scottish Shellycoat, who likes to play tricks on people and get them lost.

Goblins

These tiny terrors are usually up to no good.

Monster Stats

APPEARANCE: THEIR APPEARANCE VARIES, BUT THEY ARE USUALLY DESCRIBED AS SMALL AND UGLY

ORIGINS: EUROPEAN FOLKLORE

ALSO KNOWN AS: BOGGARTS, BOGIES, BOGLES

DANGERS: MOSTLY GENERAL MISCHIEF, BUT SOMETIMES ESCALATED TO MORE SERIOUS CRIMES, LIKE KIDNAPPING

MOST OFTEN SEEN ON: HALLOWEEN

Mischief Makers

If you venture into the dark woods of Twisted Thicket Island, you'll be chased by an army of tiny green goblins that will shoot their arrows at you. This is pretty typical goblin behavior. "Goblin" is a general term for any kind of fairy spirit that is malicious.

The evilness of a goblin can range from stealing a farmer's eggs to scaring the heck out of you—and sometimes worse. It is said that they come out on Halloween with the ghosts and try to get humans to eat fairy food, which could be a pile of acorns magically disguised to look like a delicious pie.

Beware the Redcaps!

The goblins you'll meet in the Twisted Thicket forest all wear red caps. This is the signature of a particularly evil type of goblin from Scotland that likes to dye its cap with the blood of its victims.

A "HOBGOBLIN" IS A HELPFUL GOBLIN THAT MIGHT DO CHORES AROUND YOUR HOUSE.

Trolls

Their hearts are as hard as their heads.

Monster Stats

APPEARANCE: GIANT, HAIRY, UGLY CREATURES; SOME
  STORIES SAY THEY ARE MADE OF STONE
ORIGINS: NORSE AND SCANDINAVIAN FOLKLORE
RELATED TO: OGRES
DANGERS: THEY MIGHT THROW STONES AT YOU OR STEAL
  YOUR MONEY, AND THEY HAVE BEEN KNOWN TO KILL
  HUMANS

Let's Rock!

The trolls in Twisted Thicket Island are definitely made of rocks—you can see the moss growing on their backs. Some legends say that if a troll is out in the sunlight, it will turn into a big stone statue. (In fact, this happens to the trolls in J. R. R. Tolkien's famous book *The Hobbit*.)

Troll legends can vary, depending on the country, but

the Poptropica trolls are based on Scandinavian lore. Their angry, boulder-throwing behavior is typical troll. So is their big, bulky build.

Trolling for Treasure

So why are trolls throwing rocks, anyway? Some legends say it's to keep humans away from their massive collections of gold and other treasures.

Dryads

Their lives are connected to the trees.

Why So Angry, Dryads?

In Greek mythology, a dryad is a lovely nature spirit who lives in a tree and comes out to dance in the forest with her sisters. Not so scary, right? So why are the dryads in Twisted Thicket Island chasing you like a swarm of angry bees?

They're probably riled up because they know their forest is in danger, and they don't realize you're there to help. Nature spirits are usually peaceful until their habitats are threatened, and then—watch out. Just because they're covered in bark doesn't mean they don't have any bite!

BUMMER!
A HAMADRYAD IS A TYPE OF DRYAD THAT DOESN'T LEAVE THE TREE IT LIVES IN.

Kobold

These fairies can have a split personality.

Monster Stats

APPEARANCE: ABOUT 2 FEET TALL; MIGHT HAVE GREEN SKIN, A TAIL, AND FEET INSTEAD OF HANDS

ORIGINS: EUROPEAN FOLKLORE, ESPECIALLY GERMAN

RELATED TO: GOBLINS

DANGERS: THEY CAN BE HELPFUL IF YOU TREAT THEM WELL, BUT IF NOT, THEY'LL PUSH YOU AROUND

Naughty and Nice

You won't see a kobold in Twisted Thicket Island, but you will find a kobold rune. It's named after a sometimes scary fairy that was well known in Germany.

Some kobolds were thought to live in the mines, while others were thought to live in homes. They could be helpful or harmful, depending on how you treated them. For example, if you left out a nice meal for a kobold, it might repay you by singing a lullaby to your baby. But if you forgot to feed it or give it some crusty bread, it might give you a good push.

Nokken

Whatever you do, don't go near the water . . .

Monster Stats

PRONOUNCED: NOH-KEN

APPEARANCE: SOME LEGENDS SAY IT CAN NEVER BE SEEN, BUT ARTISTS HAVE PORTRAYED IT AS A DARK, SHADOWY CREATURE WITH GLOWING EYES

ORIGINS: SCANDINAVIAN FOLKLORE

HABITAT: LAKES AND RIVERS

DANGERS: SOME NOKKEN WILL SING AT SUNRISE AND SUNSET, TRYING TO LURE PASSERSBY INTO THE WATER TO DROWN

Dark and Mysterious

Besides Sweden, the Nokken exists in many forms in Finland, Denmark, Norway, and Iceland. Water spirits in Great Britain are usually female, but the Nokken are thought to be male. They lurk in the rivers, lakes, and streams that they call home, and by most accounts their goal is to drown those who get too close.

The Nokken in Poptropica bears a resemblance to a 1904 painting of the creature by Norwegian artist Theodor Kittelsen.

POP ART

Shapeshifters?

Some stories say that spirits like the Nokken can take any form they want to. In Scotland, there is a scary water fairy called a kelpie that can take the form of a horse. If you were to climb on a kelpie on land, it would gallop off into the water, drown you, and eat you. Water fairies are known to take the form of horses in other countries, too.

Mega Monsters

What's the easiest way to make something scary? Make it really, really big! Think about it. Bunnies are adorable, right? Now imagine one the size of your house. Its cute front teeth would be the size of a door, and its huge feet could crush you in seconds. Suddenly what was once adorable is now terrifying.

Giant monsters are a natural fit for the big screen, and the 1950s were the heyday of films featuring larger-than-life creatures. They supersized everything from insects (*The Deadly Mantis*) to backyard pests (*The Killer Shrews*) to people (*Attack of the 50 Foot Woman*).

You don't have to go back to the 1950s to get an up-close look at giant creatures. In this section you'll meet some of Poptropica's most massive monsters. But first, get to know some monsters who have made a (huge) footprint on our culture.

Giant Monster Hall of Fame

King Kong: He first appeared in the 1933 film *King Kong*. A resident of Skull Island in the Pacific Ocean, he is captured by explorers and taken to New York where he falls in love, freaks out, climbs the Empire State Building, and gets shot down by planes.

Godzilla: Radiation from an atomic bomb supposedly created this reptile on steroids, who started a giant-monster craze in Japan after his first film appearance in 1954. In some films he stomps around, destroying things with his atomic breath while humans flee in terror. In others, he saves the planet from other giant monsters.

IN 1962, THE TWO MONSTERS FACED OFF IN A JAPANESE FILM, *KING KONG VS. GODZILLA.* DESPITE HIS ATOMIC-BREATH ADVANTAGE, GODZILLA LOST THE BATTLE.

Giant Spiders

Those legs, those eyes, those . . . aaaaaaaah!

Monster Stats

APPEARANCE: 8 LEGS, MULTIPLE EYES, SHARP PINCERS . . . LIKE A SPIDER, ONLY ENORMOUS

LIVES IN: EARLY POPTROPICA ISLAND, POPTROPICA GAMES

DANGERS: IN EARLY POPTROPICA, THE GIANT SPIDER IS A PIG THIEF. IN OTHER STORIES, A GIANT SPIDER WILL SPIN WEBS TO TRAP AND EAT HUMAN PREY.

Bad News for the Arachnophobic

Arachnophobia is the term for people who are afraid of spiders. Those people are afraid of the tiny spiders you encounter every day. So you can just imagine what the thought of a giant spider might do to them. Mega shivers!

In real life, the largest spider you'll ever encounter is a type of tarantula that can get as big as twelve inches across. Stories are another matter—giant spiders are very popular there.

In the Harry Potter series, a giant spider named Aragog lives in the woods. He's feared by most thanks to a reputation for snacking on humans, but Hagrid became his friend. And in the Lord of the Rings series, Gollum leads hobbits Sam and Frodo into the clutches of a giant spider named Shelob. She poisons Frodo, but Sam saves his friend before the spider can eat him.

And there are giant spiders in Poptropica, of course. The one in Early Poptropica Island is green and lives in the sewers. There's another one in Poptropica Games in the Nightcrawlers tribe common room. It won't attack you, but those cocoons all around it look suspiciously Poptropican-size.

POP
CULTURE

The word *arachnophobia*, which is a fear of spiders, comes from Arachne, a character in a Greek myth who was turned into a spider by the goddess Athena.

Don't take the time to stop and sniff these flowers—you might regret it!

Monster Stats

APPEARANCE: A HOUSEPLANT THE SIZE OF A SMALL ELEPHANT. MIGHT HAVE SHARP THORNS, VINES THAT MOVE LIKE ARMS, AND PODS THAT OPEN UP TO REVEAL SHARP TEETH.

LIVES IN: STEAMWORKS ISLAND

DANGERS: TRADITIONALLY, GIANT PLANT MONSTERS HAVE BEEN THOUGHT TO HAVE A TASTE FOR HUMANS

"Feed Me!"

If you've ever seen the movie *Little Shop of Horrors*, you'll recognize this command from the film's star, a giant, people-eating plant named Audrey II. If you want to chance an encounter with one of these creatures, then head on over to Steamworks Island.

There, you'll find that plants have come to life and are taking over the Island. There's a monster with leaves that have sharp teeth. If you make it to the end of the Island's quest, three of the most monstrous plant beasts ever created will try to stop you from succeeding. These big brutes have thick tentacle legs, eyeballs on stalks, and huge mouths dripping with slime. They're not easy to defeat—but even plant monsters have weaknesses.

Stories about plant monsters have root in facts about real-life carnivorous plants. These plants will trap insects and other very small animals and digest them with chemicals. Check out how these flesh-eating plants do it:

- **Venus flytrap:** has leaves shaped like taco shells that snap shut to trap prey inside.

- **Pitcher plant:** uses nectar to lure insects inside its tube-shaped leaves. Tiny hairs inside the tube prevent insects from climbing back out. When they get to the bottom of the tube, they slide into a pool of liquid and drown.

- **Sundew plants:** Plants in this family have long, tentacle-like leaves covered in sticky hairs that trap insects.

- **Bladderwort:** This water plant sucks prey into a bladder-like appendage. A "door" on top of the bladder shuts, and the prey is digested.

POP
SCIENCE

Pop Quiz

1. WHO WOULD WIN IN A FIGHT?
   A. A VAMPIRE
   B. A WEREWOLF
   C. FRANKENSTEIN'S MONSTER

2. WOULD YOU RATHER GET BITTEN BY . . .
   A. A ZOMBIE?
   B. A WEREWOLF?
   C. A VAMPIRE?

3. DO YOU BELIEVE
   BIGFOOT EXISTS?
   A. YES
   B. NO

4. WHICH WOULD YOU RATHER
   MEET IN A DARK ALLEY?
   A. A GOBLIN
   B. A GHOST
   C. THE JERSEY DEVIL

5. WOULD YOU RATHER . . .
   A. SEARCH FOR A CRYPTID?
   B. HUNT A VAMPIRE?
   C. SPEND A NIGHT IN A HAUNTED HOUSE?

6. WHICH FAIRY WOULD YOU
   RATHER HANG OUT WITH?
   A. A GOBLIN
   B. A TROLL
   C. A DRYAD

7. WHICH WOULD YOU RATHER
   FIND IN YOUR BACKYARD?
   A. A GIANT SPIDER
   B. A GIANT PLANT

8. DO YOU THINK THE THREAT
   OF A ZOMBIE PLAGUE IS . . .
   A. JUST AROUND THE CORNER?
   B. RIDICULOUS?
   C. INTRIGUING?

9. WHO WOULD YOU CHOOSE TO BE
   YOUR BAND'S LEAD SINGER?
   A. DRACULA
   B. A GOBLIN
   C. A NOKKEN

10. WHAT IS YOUR FAVORITE SCARY MONSTER?

Index